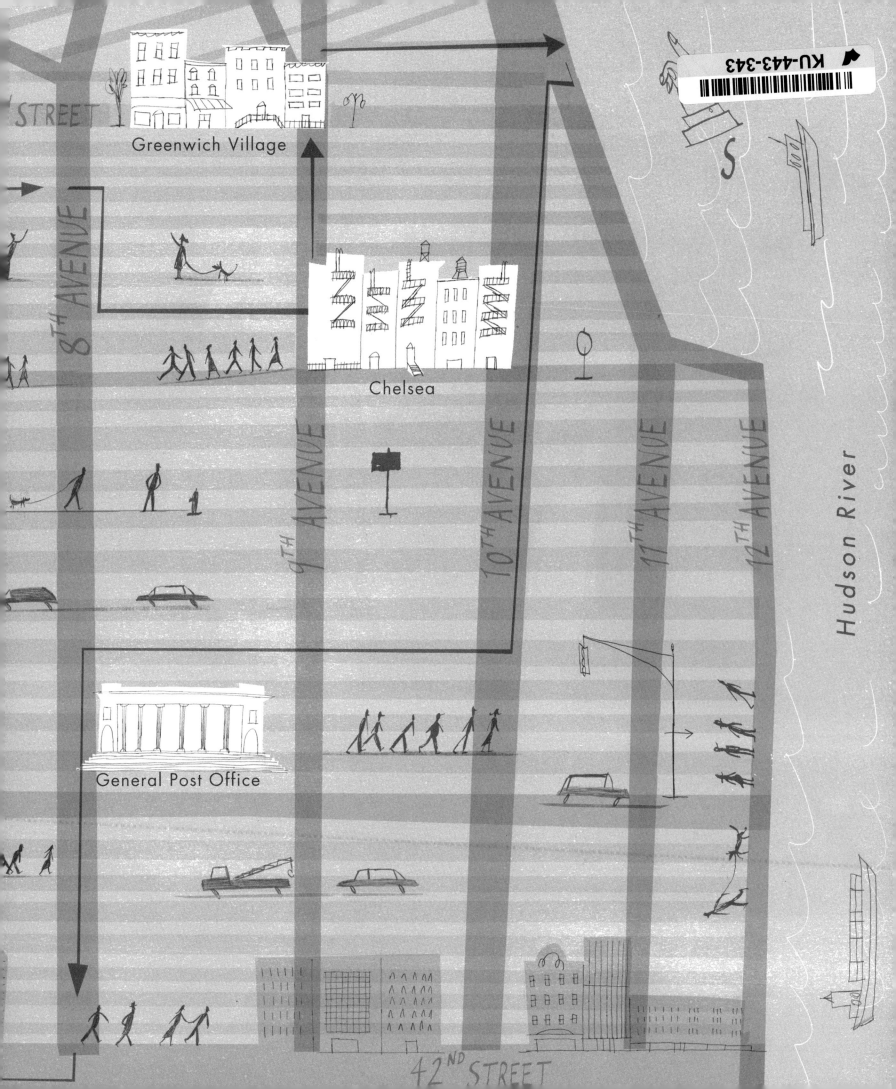

STREET

Greenwich Village

S

Chelsea

8TH AVENUE

9TH AVENUE

10TH AVENUE

11TH AVENUE

12TH AVENUE

Hudson River

General Post Office

42ND STREET

First published 2009 by Walker Books Ltd
87 Vauxhall Walk, London SE11 5HJ

8 10 9 7

With grateful thanks to Macy's Inc. for use of the Macy's name and logo
and The New York Public Library for use of the image of
the Library and its trademarked Lions

The right of Salvatore Rubbino to be identified as author and
illustrator of this work has been asserted by him in accordance
with the Copyright, Designs and Patents Act 1988

This book has been typeset in MKlang Bold and Futura Book

Printed and bound in China

British Library Cataloguing in Publication Data:
a catalogue record for this book is available from the British Library

ISBN 978-1-4063-2180-7

www.walker.co.uk

For **HAIDEE**
who waited for me
to come home

Special thanks
to
LUCY
&
BETH

A WALK IN NEW YORK

SALVATORE RUBBINO

WALKER BOOKS
AND SUBSIDIARIES
LONDON · BOSTON · SYDNEY · AUCKLAND

These trains have
all arrived from
the north.

Hello! This is **me**, and that's my dad! We've just arrived in Manhattan – the busiest part of **New York City!** Dad wants to show me round.

This platform's underground. We walk along a ramp ...

... and come up on to ground level. "Welcome to **GRAND CENTRAL**," Dad says. "The largest station in the world!"

Wow! This hall is really huge. And there are so many people – all in a hurry.

TRACK 32

TRACK 31

Grand Central has more platforms (44) and more tracks (67) than any other railway station.

8

The ceiling at Grand Central shows 2,500 stars and the constellations of the zodiac in a night sky.

The clock in the middle of Grand Central has four sides, so you can see the time wherever you are.

INFORMATION

TICKETS

About 125,000 people travel to and from Grand Central every day.

New Yorkers call
the three main areas
of Manhattan
"uptown",
"midtown"
and "downtown".

This is "midtown" where
more people work than live.

GRAND CENTRAL
TERMINAL

U.S MAIL

10

We step out onto
the street and I can't
believe my eyes!
The buildings
are so TALL.
No wonder they're
called skyscrapers.

I can tell who
the visitors are ...

we're the
ones who keep
stopping to look up!

Sailors
used
to call
ship-masts
"skyscrapers".

We stop again. This building's not as tall as it is WIDE...
Dad tells me it's the NEW YORK PUBLIC LIBRARY.
"And meet the library lions!" he says. "They guard the books inside."
Dad's silly – those lions aren't alive!

The New York Public Library opened in 1911 with a collection
of over one million books, including children's books.

NEW YOR

The library lions are called
PATIENCE and FORTITUDE.
They're made of pink marble
from Tennessee.

A librarian stops to talk to us. She says 10,000 new books come in every week and there are 88 miles of bookshelves inside!

BLIC LIBRARY

The site where the library stands used to be a reservoir.

42nd

5TH AVE

TAXI

I recognize that skyscraper! It's the
Empire State Building.

*"It has 102 floors," Dad says.
"On cloudy days you
can't see the top!"*

The Empire
State Building
isn't the
tallest building
in the world –
but it is one
of them!

NOW
OPEN

ICE COLD
DRINKS

PIZZA

NY NAILS

Deli

LEE 212
FUNG 1⅓

HOTEL
★★★

Visitors can go up the Empire State Building, so Dad and I buy tickets. A policeman shows us to a high-speed elevator ...

The Empire State Building has an observatory on the 86th floor. It's open every single day of the year.

Lift page here

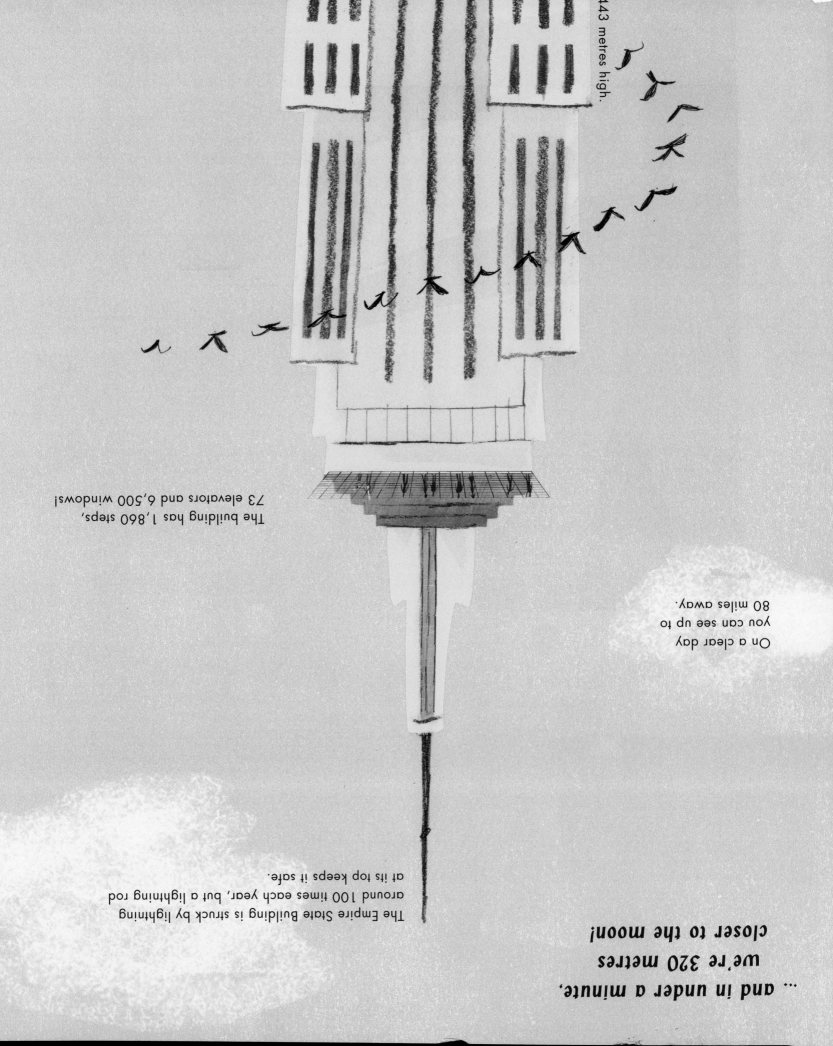

ds 443 metres high.

The building has 1,860 steps,
73 elevators and 6,500 windows!

On a clear day
you can see up to
80 miles away.

The Empire State Building is struck by lightning
around 100 times each year, but a lightning rod
at its top keeps it safe.

**... and in under a minute,
we're 320 metres
closer to the moon!**

On foggy nights in spring and autumn the lights are switched off so they won't confuse migrating birds.

From the ground to the tip of its lightning rod, the Empire State Building stan

The whole structure was built in just 410 days. It's still a record for a building of its size.

350

It's quiet up here, and water shines in all directions.
Dad tells me that Manhattan is an island.
He shows me some bridges that connect it
to New York's other boroughs.

BROOKLYN BRIDGE

MANHATTAN BRIDGE

WILLIAMSBURG
BRIDGE

New York City is made
up of five "boroughs"
or counties – Brooklyn,
Queens, the Bronx, Staten
Island and Manhattan.

I look down and the cars are tiny specks
in the ribbon streets below...

This view faces south
to New York Bay and
the Atlantic Ocean.

Back on Planet Earth, we smell a DELICIOUS smell!
But to get to the hot dog stand, we have to cross
the road! Five lanes of traffic are revving
at the lights... Dad puts me on his shoulders.
I think he thinks that I'll be safer there.

A "hot dog" is a thin sausage called
a Frankfurter put in a soft bun.
You can eat it with mustard, ketchup,
pickles, onions or just plain.

More hot dogs are eaten in New York
than anywhere else in the USA.

Macy's was one of the first shops to have big window displays.

What did you get?

That must be why their carrier bags come in so many shapes and sizes!

Now we're walking down a street called **BROADWAY**. Dad shows me an amazing skyscraper – it isn't square-shaped, it's triangular! "It's called the **Flatiron Building**," Dad says, "because it looks just like an iron."

Broadway is Manhattan's oldest, longest avenue. Its American-Indian name is the "Wickquasgeck Trail".

The Flatiron Building is one of New York's oldest sky-scrapers. It has 22 floors.

Most Manhattan streets run straight, but Broadway runs *diagonally.*

The "greenmarket" in Union Square Park sells local farmers' fresh fruit and veg.

My feet are really tired – even Dad's are – so we find
a park to rest in. It's called **UNION SQUARE PARK**.
We buy some fruit and postcards at a market stall,
then sit down in the grass and listen to the music.

George Washington was the first
president of the United States. This statue
of him on his horse is made of bronze. You can
see Washington's face on American
dollar bills and coins too.

When our energy comes back, we want to see some more.

The streets around the park are quieter and smaller. Dad says the buildings are mainly homes, not offices. People know each other, and when they talk, we hear lots of different languages...

Most people in Manhattan live in apartments.

Around 170 different languages are spoken in New York.

DON'T HONK
$ 350 PENALTY

Ciao!

Preevyet!

Ahn nyeong!

Hola!

— Ni hao!

Many old apartment buildings have iron stairways down the outside walls in case of fire, and water towers on the roof.

More people live in New York than in any other city in the USA.

Marhabah!

Salut!

TAXI

The ground under Greenwich Village is too soft to build skyscrapers on.

Most Manhattan streets are known by their numbers, but the streets in Greenwich Village usually have names.

"The Village" used to be a real village that was outside New York City.

VILLAGE CAFE

271

The more we walk now, the more we see the sky.

Dad asks me if I'm hungry. I always am!
"Let's have a snack," he says.
"This is **Greenwich Village**,
where you find the best cafes in New York!"

29

When we leave the cafe, it's nearly dark.
Dad slips down a side street and brings us to the river.
"The Hudson!" he says. "And can you see the STATUE OF LIBERTY?"

From the pier, we watch the boats, the gulls watch us
and the fishermen watch the water. The sun dips
behind the statue and
turns her crown
to gold.

About 200
different kinds
of fish live in the
Hudson River.

The statue's crown has seven rays because the world has seven seas and seven continents.

The statue is almost 93 metres high and was given to New York by the people of France in 1886.

The statue is green because it's made out of copper, which doesn't stay red unless you polish it.

Manhattan is a port. Oil, molasses, cocoa beans, grain, machinery and lots of other things pass up and down the river in ships and tanker barges.

The Hudson is a tidal river and its American-Indian name is "Muhheakautuck", which means "river that flows both ways".

"Taxi! TAXI!" Dad yells.
"Grand Central, please," I say.
Through the windows, the city
sparkles in the night.
Dad and I agree there's just
one thing better than a walk
in New York – and that's
riding a cab back!

The only way
you can catch
a New York cab
is if you hail it.

NAILS

Yankees

MAMMA'S
PIZZA

203

SHO

不豐品
大酒来

24 HR PARK

DRUG STORE

TAXI

TAXI Tax

TAXI

TAXI

More than 12,000
licenced cabs work
in New York City –
each one's
sunshine yellow!

SWIFT COMPLETION OF THEIR APPOINTED ROUNDS

The New York
General Post Office
is open 24 hours a day,
7 days a week.

At the lights, the driver
shows me one last thing.
"That's the James A. Farley Building," he says.
"It has the General Post Office inside."
He tells me what the writing carved around the top says:

"NEITHER SNOW, NOR RAIN, NOR HEAT,
NOR GLOOM OF NIGHT STAYS THESE COURIERS
FROM THE SWIFT COMPLETION OF THEIR
APPOINTED ROUNDS."

"What does it mean?" I ask.
"It's a promise that they'll do everything they can
to get your post to you," Dad says.

So when we reach the station,
I write one of our postcards
and drop it in the postbox...

POST CARD

Dear friend,
I hope one day
you'll come for
a walk in
New York too?
x x x x

To you!

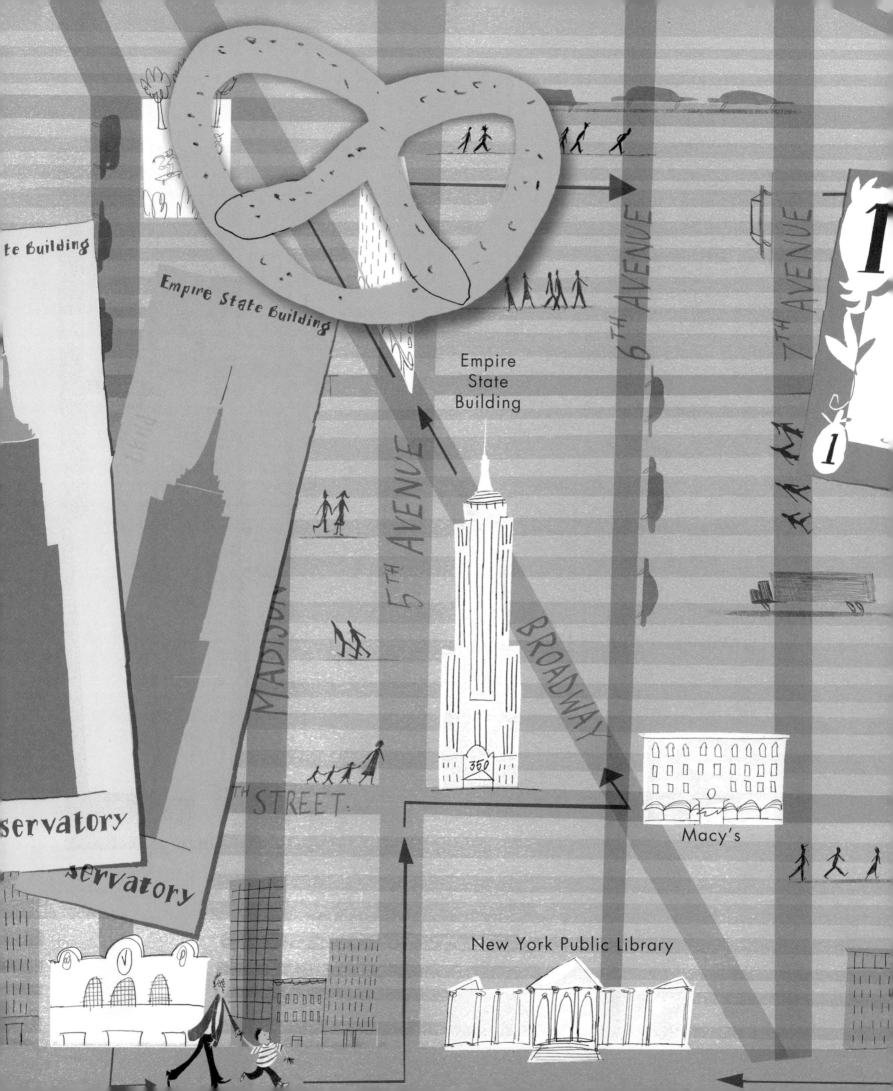

Greenwich Village

THE UNITED STATES O

ONE DOLLAR

Coffee _ _ _ _
Milkshake _ _ _ _
Cheesecake _ _ _
Chocolate
Cake _ _ _ _
Burger _ _ _ _
#2

$

Have a nice day
★ ★ ★

11TH AVENUE

12TH AVENUE

Hudson River

42ND STREET

*Salvatore Rubbino loves walking about in cities.
He always checks the weather forecast before he sets out.
"If it looks like rain," he says, "I take my umbrella – there's
nothing worse than trying to draw on soggy paper!"*

If you enjoyed this book, why not take a walk around another city!

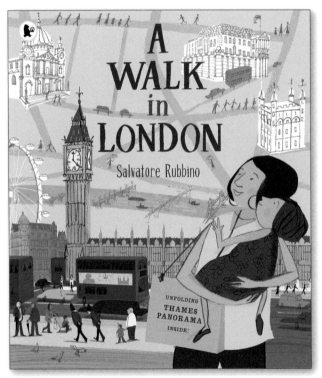
A Walk in London

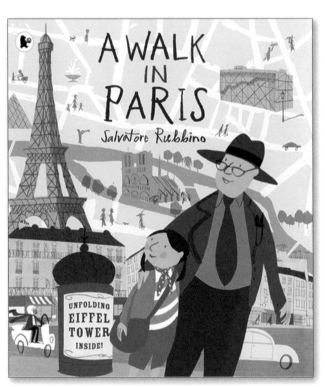
A Walk in Paris

Available from all good booksellers

www.walker.co.uk